# The New Commandment.

A

# DISCOURSE

DELIVERED

IN THE NORTH CHURCH, SALEM,

ON SUNDAY, JUNE 4, 1854.

BY O. B. FROTHINGHAM.
Pastor of the Society.

---

Published by request of the Standing Committee.

---

SALEM:
PRINTED AT THE OBSERVER OFFICE.
1854.

## PREFATORY NOTE

The author of this Discourse asks for candor on the part of his readers. He would not be understood as denying what he is obliged to omit mention of,—namely, the inestimable benefit and blessing that Christianity has been to the world; the practical good which the Church in all ages has done; and the virtues and private graces that bloom in beauty in the members of every sect, under every form of belief. He is not giving, in a single sermon, a history of the Christian Religion; but is only moved by the troubled and grievous state of the times, to reflect upon the sad and perverse mistakes of Christians, their fatal aberration from the aim of their Master, and the frightful misery and transgression resulting therefrom. Whatever else may be true, and gratefully acknowledged as being so, it is true likewise, that Christians regard their religion, *first* as a system of doctrines and *afterward* as a power of charity; and that, in consequence, the Christian Church of this country tolerates, if it does not defend and support, the Institution of Slavery, and discourages efforts to remove it. The inference is that Christianity itself is yet to be made Christian;—for Love only can remove Hate, the Spirit of Humanity alone can "heal the broken hearted, proclaim deliverance to the captives, and the opening of the prison to them that are bound, and set at liberty them that are bruised."

# DISCOURSE.

---

JOHN, xiii. 34—35. — A NEW COMMANDMENT I GIVE UNTO YOU, THAT YE LOVE ONE ANOTHER: AS I HAVE LOVED YOU, THAT YE ALSO LOVE ONE ANOTHER: BY THIS SHALL ALL MEN KNOW THAT YE ARE MY DISCIPLES, IF YE HAVE LOVE ONE TOWARD ANOTHER.

A NEW commandment this indeed! If it had ever been given before by serene philosophers to their calm disciples, met in the stillness of academic groves, when before was it ever spoken to troubled and persecuted men, by one who was hated and hunted for his life? When before was it ever addressed, amid pressing dangers, to a small band who were to array themselves against the power and wealth and infidelity of the world? When Jesus bids his disciples to love one another, he is giving them no direction of a merely politic nature, and valid for their peculiar occasion alone;—he does not say, as a military leader might to his forlorn hope,—"be united, hold together, stand fast a compact body, for union only can secure victory." The command is a permanent rule for all Christians through all time, and not only a word for an emergency. It inculcates a principle of conduct, to hold good under all circumstances, and no order of the day to be superseded by another when occasion calls for a change of tactics. All christians of whatever age, clime or condition, in life's conflict or in life's repose, are to love one another as their Master loved them; and by this token of obedience, are to be known as followers. Their relation to each other as brethren and disciples is to furnish them with motives and power sufficient to break the force of enmity, rivalry, malice and oppression, to obliterate the fanciful but prevailing distinctions of class, costume and property, to abolish the old hostility between strong and weak, wise and ignorant, rich and poor, low born and gentle, to make men sympathizers and co-workers together, full of benevolence and beneficence reciprocally in all the affairs of life. The commandment to love one another is a commandment to do all this; to consider, aid, forgive and bless one another,—even as Christ aided, forgave, and blessed us. Well might such a commandment be called *new*. How it would have amazed the listeners in any school at Athens or Rome! How it would have astonished those who sat at the feet of Gamaliel! What derision it would have called forth from the long bearded members of the Sanhedrim! What! love a publican, a fisherman, a Galilean, a Samaritan! What wonder ending in admiration did this commandment, illustrated by Christian lives, awaken among the selfish, luxurious people of Asia and Europe! A new commandment it proved itself to be, by the spell it exerted upon human discord. And were Christ to utter these words to-day in any conclave or assembly whatsoever, in any collegiate or legislative halls, in any court of justice, in any gathering for political, sectarian or even humane and religious purposes,—would they not break upon the ears of men who cared to take in their import, with all the startling force of novelty?

We talk about religious mysteries What mystery of religion is to this hour so dark and profound as this? No jargon of metaphysics puzzles the human mind half so much So impalpable is it felt to be, that men abandon all attempt to reach after it, call the effort visionary, and the result delusive, and fall back upon the ancient and approved maxims of self-seeking. And even the christian church itself, as if in despair of any general obedience of its Lord's command, limits it to the few, the "church members," so called, the "elect," and regenerate disciples. Every other mystery is thrown open to mankind, this one mystery of fraternal love is reserved for the select body of the "converted" who have been newly born from heaven. Christians themselves, in their very capacity as christians, instead of making this love of Christ the test, and sole test of discipleship, have thrown that into the background, and brought forward another, which could be more easily accepted. It is the simple truth that christians of all sects have, and still do, substantially reverse the principles of Jesus. Christianity in every existing shape, is, as professed, distinctly a system of opinions. Jesus said "Why call ye me Lord, Lord, and do not the things which I say?" His disciples of every name read the declaration backwards,—"Why do ye the things that I say, and call me not Lord, Lord?" "Speak not," Christ says, "of prophesying in my name, and casting out devils, and performing all manner of wonders;—but love your neighbor as yourselves." "Believe, believe," clamor the churches;—"believe the trinity; believe the atonement; believe the divinity of Christ; call him Lord, Lord; believe in the bible and the miracles; believe, prophecy in the name of Jesus; pray in his name;—and you need not trouble yourselves with the casting out of the demons that possess you; believe that Christ is the only Son of God. "so shall all men know that you are his disciples."

Christianity, as now existing on earth, is, I repeat, a system of metaphysics. Men consider that their belief,—their opinions, well or ill founded,—their notions, crude, blind, prejudiced though they may be, will ensure for them the blessing of Christ, however atrocious be the deeds they do, however unloving the dispositions they entertain. The christian church is builded on human philosophy, and its extension is but the extension of one or another form of philosophy. Every sect has its unalterable and saving creed; the spread of christianity is but the multiplication of sects, and therefore the multiplication of creeds. Each new branch of the vine, has been a new heresy. The spirit of contention, and not the spirit of charity, has distributed christian communities far and wide, and planted churches in every part of the earth. Each denomination represents a quarrel; and how many congregations owe their existence to a feud? How many spires are pushed up into the skies out of spite? So it has ever been. Had all the time that has been spent in discussing christian dogmas been devoted to doing christian deeds, the earth would present a very different aspect from that which it presents now. We might have fewer sects, but we should have fewer miseries and sins. We might not have so many churches, but we should have, in greater abundance, the spirit of Christ. But christians care more for dogmas than they do for charity; and are ready to quarrel and persecute, and hate one another, and to utterly eradicate the spirit of their master in their zeal to make valid a distinction, or to establish a quibble.

Christendom, alas, that we must confess it! is a group of hostile sectarian schools, debating their problems of philosophy in a temper of bitterness, which make of one body many members, instead of making of many members one body. This is no exaggerated or heated statement. All know that in every existing denomination, not excepting the most liberal, a creed is the test of discipleship; all know that the wars of the creeds have created and multiplied sects, sectarian establishments, churches, congregations and preachers;—all know that christian operations are all but universally sectarian, in their basis and purpose, and that the burden of christian instruction is controversial and dogmatical; all know that the relation of the sects of christendom to each other, is and ever has been one of jealousy and hostility, to such a degree that the hatred of theologians has passed into a proverb; that individual christians, always join battle first upon points of faith, and if they cannot agree here, will break an already existing friendship, and violate the dearest ties of kindred;—all know that for every ten who will listen to a discourse of charity, a hundred will throng to hear a preacher of polemics, and that for each dollar given to the cause of brotherly kindness, ten are contributed to diffuse the doctrine of the sect. Must we not then confess that credence is put before love, that belief is made the test of discipleship, and that christians by the very best evidence of conduct, declare that they may safely be guilty of "malice, hatred and uncharitableness," provided they are sound in philosophy?

It is on dogmatical grounds generally that men unite themselves with christian churches and societies. It does seem as if at this epoch of the church, christians might agree to differ upon matters of mere speculation, and might believe enough of the substance of faith to make subordinate its diversities of form. Cannot men who love one another as Christ loved them, worship with a single heart the living God, without regard to the subtle definitions of Him that haunt the secret hiding places of the brain? Cannot persons who love one another as Christ loved them, love and serve their common master according to his own direction and bidding, undisturbed by the arbitrary theories which they may severally entertain respecting his interior nature? Unhappily it seems to be impossible. We must all believe alike, though in the effort to produce the required intellectual conformity, the most violent injustice be done to christian feeling and to christian principle. Oh! how new even to-day, is the commandment to love one another! Persons are not even admitted to the communion, save in very few churches, however pure and self-sacrificing of heart, if they have a reasonable doubt upon any point of the creed; and how rarely does it happen that any are forbidden the communion by reason of a base and ignoble life? It seems often as if but for the stimulus of quarrel and controversy the institution of religion would decline. A friend said to me, not long since, "what would become of the churches if it were not for these dogmas you complain of? It is only as sectarians that people go to meeting. They go, not out of love to God, but out of disagreement with man. They go in the spirit of unbelief, and not in the spirit of belief; they go to hear their opinions echoed, and the opinions of others confuted; and if all people believed alike, or ranked belief among secondary things, the mission chapels would be empty, the meeting houses closed, and the sanctuaries deserted." It was a hard saying and far too sweeping, but it sunk like lead upon my heart, as I thought how near it came to the truth.

"By this shall all men know that ye are my disciples, if ye have love one toward another." We can scarcely credit the fact that these words were spoken by the founder of a religion which has accepted a principle directly opposed to their spirit and even to their letter; a religion which, it is scarcely too much to say, has built itself up, and extended itself, by making of secondary importance what the Master placed first, and ranking among the incidental effects of faith, what he declared to be its efficient and permanent cause. How strange a commentary does christian history furnish upon the idea of Christ! How plainly does it prove that christians may be guilty of any atrocity, if they only hold fast the faith, and that the purest life can save none who have incurred the slightest taint of heresy.

In 1179, Pope Alexander III. convened the *Third Council of Lateran*, for the purpose of establishing new canons of discipline and morality for the church of Christ;—no doubt a most needful work. At these councils the most learned and influential of the christian fathers assembled, and the Holy Spirit was expected to preside. Surely no more solemn call could be issued than this, in an age of wars and wiles, to make new rules of discipline and morality for the christian church. And what was done? Why the main business was the condemnation of sundry sects of christians, including the Albigenses, and the last canon stated, that although the church abhors the shedding of blood, it does not refuse the countenance and support of the temporal laws of christian princes, because the fear of corporal punishment is sometimes efficacious in producing spiritual reformation. And who were the Albigenses? They were a class of christians in the South of France, unobtrusive and simple people, of extreme purity of faith and life, approaching more nearly than any other religious body to christians of the earliest centuries; but as they did not recognize the authority of the pope, it was decided in general council to be an act of christian *morality*, not to bring a number of them to Rome to purify the ecclesiastics, but to pronounce them accursed and to waken persecution against them. Shortly after the breaking up of this Council, and as one of its results, followed the crusade against the Albigenses. The cross, on which the Saviour suffered, laying down his life for mankind, was blazoned as an emblem in blood red letters upon coats of mail, and gave shape to the sword hilts of warriors, and he was best known as a disciple, who dyed both redder in his brother's gore. No more merciless persecution is recorded in history than this. Every sort of ferocity was practised; the war raged for twenty years; the Albigenses were extirpated in France; the country was devastated; the very language and poetry of the Troubadours became extinct, and whatever of justice and humanity there was, was trodden out also under the iron heels of the soldiery. Yet these men were Christians; these bigoted prelates and pitiless nobles were Christians; these exterminating decrees were uttered in the very name of Christ; these exterminating lances were levelled in his honor; no one doubted that. Where was the new commandment then? The inspired church had never discovered among its articles of faith this one which should have led them all. The doctrine of papal supremacy was more vital than the precept, "Love one another as I have loved you." Jesus *cured* people as a means of spiritual reformation,—his disciples put them to the sword.

But this was in the Catholic church. The Protestants have done no better. The new commandment was as unintelligible to the Protestants as to the Catholics. Take another instance. "The Westminster Assembly of learned and godly Divines," convened in 1643, and continued in session more than five years. Its members were among the wisest, gravest and best of men, seriously intent upon promoting the interests of the church, and their meetings, eleven hundred and sixty-three in number, were characterized by the utmost order and decorum. They produced a Directory of Worship, a Confession of Calvinistic Faith, a Form of Church Government, and two Catehisms, in-inculcating earnestly the duties of public worship, reading of Scriptures, private and domestic prayer, and setting forth a complete system of practical duty, drawn chiefly from the Old Testament. But in the very midst of their sessions, the Presbyterian party, being in the ascendancy, brought forward and passed an ordinance against blasphemy and heresy, which enacted that for certain specified offences under this head, if the party on trial should not abjure his error, or having abjured, should relapse, he should suffer death, as in case of "felony, without benefit of clergy." Fortunately, the sword of the civil magistrate was not in the hands of ecclesiastics, to execute this ordinance; but the heart to execute it was here. Where was the "new commandment" then? And how new would the commandment, "Love one another, as I have loved you," have appeared in those days. Men's eyes were not open to read it. They thought themselves as good Christians, and better, for their intolerance and hate, because it showed how completely they had surrendered themselves up, heart and soul, to the demands of their creed.*

---

* In 1644, a tract was printed, entitled, "Wholesome Severity reconciled with Christian Liberty, or the True Resolution of the present Controversy concerning Liberty of Conscience." Among other things the author says,—"Under these fair colors and handsome pretexts, (namely, of Equity and Brotherly Love,) do Sectaries infuse their poison, I mean their pernicious, God-provoking, Truth-defacing, Church-ruinating, and State-shaking Toleration. The plain English of the question is this,—Whether the Christian magistrate be keeper of both

But this was long ago. True; but things are substantially not much better now. The most liberal body of believers in our own community has excluded from the company of disciples, one whose faithful, humane and spotless life, would honor any Christian fraternity, because he differs from them in opinion on some points of historical criticism and speculative theology. The Christian Church universal of this country,—I state but a common place truth,—is blind and indifferent to the most hideous institution now existing under the sun; an institution which, on an enormous scale, outrages human rights and crushes human nature—which indeed has been truly said, and long ago, and by one himself entangled with it, to comprise in itself literally or by implication, every species of iniquity and wrong. It is notorious that the Churches in the Southern States, one and all, apologize for slavery and defend it from the Bible; and that the Northern Churches, with here and there an insignificant exception, are silent upon it, tacitly give their influence in its favor, openly rebuke every attempt to expose its enormity,—and too often plead for it as once at least sanctioned by divine and by apostolical authority. The persons who engage in the effort to abolish the institution of slavery are, for the most part, unconnected with the Church;—

---

tables; whether he ought to suppress his own enemies, but not God's enemies; and preserve his own ordinances, but not *Christ's ordinances*, from violation," etc. And another writer delivers himself thus:—"A Toleration is the grand design of the Devil, his master piece, and chief engine he works by at this time, to uphold his tottering kingdom; it is the most compendious, ready and sure way to destroy all religion, lay all waste, and bring in all evil; it is a most transcendant, Catholic, and fundamental evil for the kingdom of any that can be imagined: as original sin is the most fundamental sin—all sin—having the seed and spawn of all in it; so a Toleration hath all errors in it, and all evils."

and there is too much truth in the saying, that the church has been the great obstacle in the way of this movement of humanity. But the churches of this country deem themselves no less christian on this account. Nay, they regard themselves as all the more, and all the more *peculiarly* christian, in their indifference to philanthropic enterprise.—Christianity, we are told, is a scheme of redemption for the miraculous regeneration of human souls; the Christain is one who holds the orthodox faith, believing in the supernatural being and power, and in the vicarious merits of Christ; and it is the duty of the church to explain and defend its doctrines, to bring people to its sacraments, and make them assent to its creeds. The great company of disciples, which is the body of Christ, have nothing to do with the abolition of those evils which express human rage and hatred, and ordain malice, pride and selfishness as permanent institutions of society. But where then is the new commandment? and what becomes of the Savior's test of discipleship?

Last week was anniversary week, the "Holy Week of the churches." Boston was full of christian divines, assembled in their several conventions, to discuss the interests of their religion. Every sect was represented; the meeting houses were thronged from morning till night. Prayer was ceaseless, preaching was incessant. The Bible Societies, Sunday School Societies, Missionary Societies, held high counsel. There were theological discourses of every shade, all bristling with the most approved dialectics. Metaphysics held their orgies.—While thus the people were streaming to and fro, hymn book and prayer book in hand, while the doctors were disputing about Trinity and Unity, Christ and the Holy Spirit, Original Sin and Atonement, duties to the Hindoos and the Cherokees, the best mode of instructing children in the doctrines of the Gospel, and gathering them into the fold of Christ;—in the very centre of the city, in the very halls of christian Justice, *Christ himself*, in the person of one of the least of his disciples, was arraigned before Pontius Pilate. There sate the procurator on his tribunal; there were the mercenary soldiery, filling the avenues, and desecrating the halls of the Temple of Justice, and polluting the very air of the sacred chamber with their foul presence; there were the hired ruffians, from the sinks and kennels of the town, stalking insolently up and down before the seat at which they should have been arraigned as malefactors; there stood the prisoner bound and guarded; and what was his crime? Why: he had declared himself a *king*; the king of his own person; he had asserted his absolute dominion over his own limbs,—his own regal autocracy of will,—his natural right to come and go as he would. "Art thou such a king?" he is asked. "I am a king." Then come the false witnesses with their testimony. Some kindly persons will compromise, buying him off with money. A message arrives from the Southern head quarters, saying, "if thou let this man go, thou art not Cæsar's friend." The multitude clamor without, this time however, that the prisoner be released, and that Barabbas be given up. All this goes forward in broad day, for successive days, in a city crowded with people who had come up to the great passover festival. The prisoner is condemned; and ere that mighty concourse of pious christians has dispersed, his insulted form, manacled and guarded by nearly two thousand armed men, is led along our modern *via dolorosa*, toward the place of infamy and pain beyond the city. What a commentary this upon the christianity of christendom; the christianity of the puritan city, the "Paradise of divines!" So once more has Christ been delivered over to his tormentors to be scourged and crucified. Once more has the purple robe been flung upon him, and the sceptre of reeds been placed in his hand. Once more in the holy city, at holy time, amid circumstances brutal and insulting as at first, has the form of a man, made in the image of Christ, been sold to an ignominious doom. Where was the church? Where was the body of disciples? Where was the new commandment? The church was settling its own matters; and the disciples were engaged in saying "Lord, Lord," in churches and vestry meetings; and the new commandment was too new to have come to their knowledge. Did they not call one another brothers and sisters at the communion table, and was not that enough?

But, brethren, what are we to do with this new commandment? There it stands, unrepealed, in all its significance. "As I have loved you, love ye also one another; by this shall all men know that ye are my disciples, if ye have love one toward another." "*As I have loved you.*" Yes, as I have loved the poor and outcast, and persecuted and defenceless, and laid down my life for them; so love ye one another. I know this is a hard commandment, and hard to be obeyed. But are we at liberty then to disobey it, or to set it aside? I know that Christian love is no mere emotion, or impulse — no passionate or tender feeling of commiseration for the unfortunate. I know that it is a high and solemn principle, thoughtful and comprehensive,—that it embraces *all*, the sinner as well as the sinned against, the persecutor as well as his victim, the master and the slave alike; that it is never violent or vindictive, never makes kindness towards one justify cruelty toward another. I know all this very well; but because love is not *all* pity, shall we say it is not pity? because it bids us bless the persecutor as well as the victim, shall we say it does not bid us bless the victim? Because we cannot keep the whole law at once, shall we excuse ourselves from keeping any of it? The whole duty under the new commandment is not offered to us at one and the same moment, and we must meet it as it comes, fulfilling it in its most obvious sense first; by obedience to the easiest, learning to obey the hardest. But how, even then, can we fulfill it at all? it is asked. What could we have done in a case like this of last week? What could Jesus himself have done had he been there? I cannot tell. It is enough, that where there is a will, there is a way. Questions of conduct are always perplexing, even in trifling matters. No one can judge for another. Modes of action must differ with individual minds and characters. But the motive which shall prompt to action of some kind may be the same in all. Modes of action are suggested by the intellect and judgment; and must vary widely as these. Motives of action spring from the heart and conscience, which are common to all mankind. One thing we all can do: we can *feel* as Christians should; if we *feel not*, we can do nothing; and it is because we feel not, that we do nothing. And after all, feeling *is* doing. Feeling *will* express itself in characteristic ways. What is in us *must* come out of us. If nothing comes out of us, there is nothing in us. If the effect we produce be evil, it is vain to pretend that the cause that produces it is good; that pity expresses itself in indifference, mercy in callousness, and humanity in inhuman allegiance to inhuman statutes. Judge the tree by its fruits. If but one in a thousand of those nominal and professing Christians in Boston had been a *real* Christian, that strange, that hideous outrage never could have been perpetrated; the law never could have been executed; the infamous statute never would have overridden the new commandment. Without a blow struck, without a hand lifted, the power of the government would have fallen down and expired, unable to breathe in that atmosphere of humane feeling. No commissioner would have issued a warrant of arrest; no officer would have served it, policemen would have resigned their trusts; the military would have disbanded, rather than array themselves in such a cause; no wharf, no ship, no carriage or conveyance of any kind would have been furnished for the unholy work. The slave hunter would have been an outlaw, denied shelter, food, service,—proscribed, avoided in the streets, pointed at as an enemy of his kind. The foot of the intruder would have found no resting place, the blight of an unuttered and unutterable indignation would have fallen upon his heart, the slow, unmoving finger of scorn would have pointed him his way back to the place whence he came. Had Boston been full of real Christians the last week, a virtue would have gone out from it, which the slave owner could neither have resisted nor met; he never would have dared to seek his victim in a Christian city, full of Christian divines on the Holy Week of the year.

One thing, brethren, I am here earnestly to say,—that this new commandment sums up our Christian duty, and defines the conditions of discipleship. "By this shall all men know that ye are my disciples, if ye have love one toward another." Nothing can be plainer. To forget the commandment, whatever else we may remember, is to forget Christ; to abuse it is to abuse Christ; to deny it is to deny Christ. Let this be distinctly understood. According to the express declaration of the founder of our religion, we are Christians, just so far as we heed this new commandment, and no farther. Were this clearly seen and comprehended, I believe that the state of our public affairs would wear altogether a new aspect. In our community there is a deep and wide love of religion, as religion is understood. Our people have a profound respect for what they consider to be Christianity. If their faith is rudely assailed, their formulary of doctrine denied, their Bible insulted, or their worship disturbed, they express the utmost horror and indignation; they do not spare the blasphemer of their dogmatic Christ, or the impugner of their inspired creed. But a wolf may enter the very fold of Christ and take away one of the sheep, and they have nothing to say. If a law were to be passed, denying to our people the privilege of worshipping God according to the dictates of their consciences, prescribing a service book or a set of authorized articles, they would break out into open rebellion; they would raise the cry of blasphemy, and in the name of God would make the edict of no effect, and if necessary would trample it under their foot. But a law has been passed bidding them send one of their brethren back to the scourge and sorrow of bondage; and they make it a Christian duty to obey, and will violate a great many other Christian duties in order to fulfill this one.

Let it now be understood that this is Christianity; that the new commandment defines the conditions of discipleship; that none are Christians, or can inherit the blessings and privileges of Christians, who do not feel the force and endeavor to enact the purport of this; let it be once understood that it is vain to call Christ "Lord, Lord," if we do not the things which he says; — and the whole force of moral and religious feeling that now is so watchful and mighty against the encroachments and assaults of unbelief, would turn and concentrate its awful power against injustice and inhumanity, and in a whirlwind of indignation would sweep away oppression and oppression's edicts from the land. Let Christianity be not a dogma any longer, but an obedient and humane life, and the thing is done. But so long as we fetter with bands of metaphysics and confine in churches and sacramental rites, the only power that can possibly overcome iniquity, the cause of Christ is desperate indeed.

Here, my friends, is the simple issue. The cause of humanity—the anti-slavery cause—is the cause of Christ, inasmuch as it involves directly, and in all its applications, the principles of brotherly love. In every scourged and vilified slave, I see the person of the crucified. Over against every statute, signed by the President, and enforced by legal penalties, is set the new commandment uttered by the Christ, and enforced by the more dreadful penalties which the divine laws of the universe visit upon transgression. The former must be explained, and argued and defended anew, on each occasion of its application. The latter is easily comprehended ; each heart knows it to be true ; each conscience upholds it, and nothing but deceit and self-seeking can set it aside. And if we would learn how to fulfill it, we have but to think how Christ loved *all*, loved them and died for them ; we have but to put him in the position of every poor, forsaken, distressed, persecuted and injured man,—in the place of the beaten and crucified slave,—and then remember the words he spake, —" *Inasmuch as ye did it not unto one of the least of these, ye did it not unto me.*"

www.ingramcontent.com/pod-product-compliance
Lightning Source LLC
LaVergne TN
LVHW020636110826
845149LV00004B/1226

* 9 7 8 1 4 1 8 1 9 1 4 1 2 *